50 Warm Meals for Cold Days

By: Kelly Johnson

Table of Contents

- Classic Beef Stew
- Chicken and Dumplings
- Tomato Basil Soup
- Creamy Potato Leek Soup
- Chicken Pot Pie
- Beef Chili
- French Onion Soup
- Baked Ziti
- Lasagna
- Mac and Cheese with Bacon
- Shrimp and Grits
- Roast Chicken with Vegetables
- Shepherd's Pie
- Cornbread and Chili
- Vegetable Minestrone
- Creamy Butternut Squash Soup
- Clam Chowder

- Baked Potato Soup
- Chicken Tortilla Soup
- Pulled Pork Sandwiches
- Beef and Vegetable Stir-Fry
- Meatball Soup
- Beef Stroganoff
- Beef and Barley Soup
- Sweet Potato and Black Bean Chili
- Sausage and Pepper Skillet
- Chicken Alfredo
- Chicken and Rice Casserole
- Beef and Mushroom Pie
- Stuffed Bell Peppers
- Chicken and Wild Rice Soup
- Lasagna Soup
- Spaghetti Carbonara
- Pork Tenderloin with Apples
- Risotto with Parmesan and Mushrooms
- Chicken Parmesan

- Baked Macaroni and Cheese
- Fish Tacos with Cilantro Lime Rice
- Spicy Sausage Soup
- Braised Short Ribs
- Cajun Jambalaya
- Chili Mac
- Chicken and Sweet Potato Skillet
- Beef and Potato Casserole
- Shrimp Scampi
- Vegetable Curry
- Meatball Sub Sandwiches
- Eggplant Parmesan
- Pork Carnitas
- Beef Tacos with Guacamole

Classic Beef Stew

Ingredients

- 2 lbs beef stew meat, cubed
- 2 tbsp olive oil
- 1 onion, chopped
- 2 cloves garlic, minced
- 4 cups beef broth
- 2 cups water
- 3 carrots, sliced
- 3 potatoes, peeled and diced
- 2 celery stalks, chopped
- 2 bay leaves
- 1 tsp dried thyme
- 1 tsp dried rosemary
- Salt and pepper to taste
- 2 tbsp cornstarch (optional, for thickening)

Instructions

1. In a large pot, heat the olive oil over medium heat. Brown the beef stew meat in batches, then set aside.
2. In the same pot, sauté the onion and garlic until soft, about 3-4 minutes.

3. Return the beef to the pot. Add the beef broth, water, carrots, potatoes, celery, bay leaves, thyme, and rosemary. Bring to a boil.

4. Reduce heat to low, cover, and simmer for 1.5-2 hours, or until the beef and vegetables are tender.

5. If you'd like a thicker stew, mix the cornstarch with a little cold water and stir it into the stew. Simmer for 5 more minutes until thickened.

6. Season with salt and pepper to taste before serving.

Chicken and Dumplings

Ingredients

- 4 cups chicken broth
- 2 cups cooked, shredded chicken
- 1 onion, chopped
- 2 cloves garlic, minced
- 1 cup carrots, diced
- 2 celery stalks, chopped
- 2 cups all-purpose flour
- 2 tsp baking powder
- 1/2 tsp salt
- 1/2 tsp pepper
- 1/2 tsp dried thyme
- 1/2 cup milk
- 1/4 cup unsalted butter, melted
- 1/4 cup fresh parsley, chopped

Instructions

1. In a large pot, bring the chicken broth to a simmer. Add the shredded chicken, onion, garlic, carrots, and celery. Simmer until the vegetables are tender, about 10 minutes.

2. In a bowl, mix the flour, baking powder, salt, pepper, and thyme.

3. Add the milk and melted butter to the dry ingredients, stirring until just combined.

4. Drop spoonfuls of the dumpling batter into the simmering broth, covering the pot with a lid.

5. Cook the dumplings for 10-12 minutes, until they are cooked through and fluffy.

6. Stir in the fresh parsley and season with salt and pepper to taste. Serve hot.

Tomato Basil Soup

Ingredients

- 2 tbsp olive oil
- 1 onion, chopped
- 2 cloves garlic, minced
- 2 cans (14.5 oz each) diced tomatoes
- 2 cups vegetable broth
- 1 tsp dried basil
- 1/2 tsp sugar
- Salt and pepper to taste
- 1/2 cup heavy cream
- Fresh basil for garnish

Instructions

1. In a large pot, heat the olive oil over medium heat. Add the onion and garlic, cooking until soft and fragrant, about 5 minutes.
2. Add the diced tomatoes, vegetable broth, basil, sugar, salt, and pepper. Bring to a simmer and cook for 15-20 minutes.
3. Use an immersion blender to blend the soup until smooth. Alternatively, carefully blend in batches using a regular blender.
4. Stir in the heavy cream and cook for an additional 5 minutes.
5. Garnish with fresh basil and serve hot.

Creamy Potato Leek Soup

Ingredients

- 2 tbsp butter
- 2 leeks, cleaned and sliced
- 2 cloves garlic, minced
- 4 cups chicken broth
- 4 cups potatoes, peeled and diced
- 1 cup heavy cream
- Salt and pepper to taste
- Fresh parsley for garnish

Instructions

1. In a large pot, melt the butter over medium heat. Add the leeks and garlic, cooking until softened, about 5 minutes.

2. Add the chicken broth and diced potatoes. Bring to a boil, then reduce the heat and simmer for 15-20 minutes until the potatoes are tender.

3. Use an immersion blender to blend the soup until smooth, or carefully blend in batches in a regular blender.

4. Stir in the heavy cream and cook for 5 more minutes.

5. Season with salt and pepper to taste, and garnish with fresh parsley before serving.

Chicken Pot Pie

Ingredients

- 2 cups cooked, shredded chicken
- 2 cups frozen peas and carrots
- 1 cup celery, chopped
- 1 cup onion, chopped
- 2 tbsp butter
- 1/4 cup all-purpose flour
- 2 cups chicken broth
- 1/2 cup heavy cream
- 1 tsp dried thyme
- Salt and pepper to taste
- 1 package refrigerated pie crusts (or homemade)

Instructions

1. Preheat the oven to 400°F.
2. In a large pan, melt the butter over medium heat. Add the onion and celery, cooking until soft, about 5 minutes.
3. Stir in the flour and cook for 2-3 minutes to form a roux.
4. Gradually whisk in the chicken broth and heavy cream, simmering until the mixture thickens.

5. Stir in the shredded chicken, peas, carrots, thyme, salt, and pepper. Remove from heat.

6. Roll out the pie crusts and place one into a 9-inch pie dish. Fill with the chicken mixture and cover with the second pie crust. Trim the edges and pinch to seal.

7. Cut a few slits in the top crust to allow steam to escape.

8. Bake for 30-35 minutes, until the crust is golden brown. Let cool for a few minutes before serving.

Beef Chili

Ingredients

- 1 lb ground beef
- 1 onion, chopped
- 2 cloves garlic, minced
- 1 can (14.5 oz) diced tomatoes
- 1 can (15 oz) kidney beans, drained
- 1 can (15 oz) black beans, drained
- 1 tbsp chili powder
- 1 tsp ground cumin
- 1/2 tsp smoked paprika
- Salt and pepper to taste
- Shredded cheddar cheese, sour cream, and chopped green onions for topping

Instructions

1. In a large pot, cook the ground beef over medium heat until browned. Remove excess fat.
2. Add the onion and garlic and cook for another 5 minutes, until softened.
3. Stir in the diced tomatoes, kidney beans, black beans, chili powder, cumin, paprika, salt, and pepper.
4. Bring to a simmer and cook for 30-40 minutes, stirring occasionally.

5. Serve with shredded cheddar cheese, sour cream, and chopped green onions as toppings.

French Onion Soup

Ingredients

- 4 large onions, thinly sliced
- 3 tbsp butter
- 2 cloves garlic, minced
- 6 cups beef broth
- 1/2 cup white wine
- 1 tsp dried thyme
- Salt and pepper to taste
- 1 baguette, sliced
- 2 cups shredded Gruyère cheese

Instructions

1. In a large pot, melt the butter over medium heat. Add the onions and cook, stirring occasionally, for 40-45 minutes, until the onions are caramelized and golden brown.
2. Add the garlic and cook for another 1-2 minutes.
3. Pour in the white wine, scraping the bottom of the pot to release any brown bits. Let the wine reduce by half.
4. Add the beef broth, thyme, salt, and pepper. Bring to a simmer and cook for 20-30 minutes.
5. Meanwhile, toast the baguette slices.

6. Ladle the soup into bowls, top with a slice of toasted baguette, and sprinkle with Gruyère cheese.

7. Place the bowls under the broiler for 2-3 minutes until the cheese is melted and bubbly.

Baked Ziti

Ingredients

- 1 lb ziti pasta
- 2 cups marinara sauce
- 1 lb ricotta cheese
- 2 cups shredded mozzarella cheese
- 1/2 cup grated Parmesan cheese
- 1 tsp dried basil
- 1 tsp dried oregano
- Salt and pepper to taste

Instructions

1. Preheat the oven to 375°F.
2. Cook the ziti pasta according to the package instructions. Drain and set aside.
3. In a large bowl, mix the cooked pasta, marinara sauce, ricotta cheese, mozzarella cheese, Parmesan cheese, basil, oregano, salt, and pepper.
4. Transfer the mixture to a baking dish and spread evenly.
5. Bake for 25-30 minutes, until the cheese is melted and bubbly.
6. Serve hot and garnish with extra Parmesan if desired.

Lasagna

Ingredients

- 12 lasagna noodles
- 2 lbs ground beef
- 1 onion, chopped
- 2 cloves garlic, minced
- 2 cups marinara sauce
- 15 oz ricotta cheese
- 2 cups shredded mozzarella cheese
- 1/2 cup grated Parmesan cheese
- 1 egg
- 1 tsp dried basil
- 1 tsp dried oregano
- Salt and pepper to taste

Instructions

1. Preheat the oven to 375°F.
2. Cook the lasagna noodles according to the package instructions. Drain and set aside.
3. In a large skillet, cook the ground beef, onion, and garlic until browned. Drain excess fat.

4. Stir in the marinara sauce, basil, oregano, salt, and pepper. Simmer for 10-15 minutes.

5. In a separate bowl, mix the ricotta cheese, egg, and half of the mozzarella cheese.

6. In a large baking dish, layer the noodles, meat sauce, and cheese mixture. Repeat until all ingredients are used.

7. Top with the remaining mozzarella and Parmesan cheese.

8. Bake for 30-40 minutes, until the cheese is golden and bubbly. Let cool for 10 minutes before serving.

Mac and Cheese with Bacon

Ingredients

- 1 lb elbow macaroni
- 4 slices bacon
- 2 cups shredded sharp cheddar cheese
- 1 cup shredded mozzarella cheese
- 1/4 cup butter
- 1/4 cup all-purpose flour
- 2 cups milk
- 1/2 cup heavy cream
- Salt and pepper to taste
- 1/2 tsp garlic powder
- 1/2 tsp onion powder
- 1/4 cup breadcrumbs (optional for topping)

Instructions

1. Cook the macaroni according to package instructions, then drain and set aside.
2. In a large skillet, cook the bacon over medium heat until crispy. Remove the bacon and set aside, reserving the bacon fat in the skillet.
3. In the same skillet, melt the butter in the bacon fat. Add the flour and whisk to create a roux. Cook for 1-2 minutes.

4. Gradually add the milk and heavy cream, whisking constantly to avoid lumps. Cook until the sauce thickens, about 5-7 minutes.

5. Stir in the shredded cheddar and mozzarella cheese until melted and smooth. Season with salt, pepper, garlic powder, and onion powder.

6. Add the cooked macaroni to the cheese sauce, stirring to combine.

7. Crumble the bacon and stir it into the mac and cheese, or sprinkle it on top for serving.

8. If desired, sprinkle breadcrumbs on top and bake at 350°F for 10-15 minutes to create a crispy topping.

9. Serve hot and enjoy!

Shrimp and Grits

Ingredients

- 1 lb large shrimp, peeled and deveined
- 1 cup stone-ground grits
- 4 cups water or chicken broth
- 2 tbsp butter
- 1/2 cup heavy cream
- 2 tbsp olive oil
- 2 cloves garlic, minced
- 1 tbsp lemon juice
- 1/2 tsp paprika
- Salt and pepper to taste
- 1/4 cup green onions, chopped
- 1/4 cup crumbled bacon (optional)

Instructions

1. Bring the water or chicken broth to a boil in a medium pot. Add the grits, reduce the heat to low, and cook, stirring occasionally, for 20-25 minutes, until the grits are tender and creamy. Stir in the butter and heavy cream, and season with salt and pepper.

2. While the grits are cooking, heat the olive oil in a large skillet over medium heat. Add the garlic and cook for 1 minute until fragrant.

3. Add the shrimp to the skillet, seasoning with paprika, salt, and pepper. Cook for 2-3 minutes per side, or until the shrimp are pink and opaque.

4. Stir in the lemon juice and cook for an additional 1 minute.

5. Serve the shrimp over the creamy grits, garnished with green onions and crumbled bacon if desired.

Roast Chicken with Vegetables

Ingredients

- 1 whole chicken (about 4 lbs)
- 2 tbsp olive oil
- 1 lemon, halved
- 4 cloves garlic, smashed
- 1 onion, quartered
- 2 carrots, peeled and cut into chunks
- 2 potatoes, peeled and cut into chunks
- 1 sprig fresh rosemary
- 1 sprig fresh thyme
- Salt and pepper to taste

Instructions

1. Preheat the oven to 425°F.
2. Pat the chicken dry with paper towels. Rub the chicken with olive oil, and season generously with salt and pepper, inside and out.
3. Stuff the chicken with the lemon halves, garlic, onion, and herbs. Tie the legs together with kitchen twine.
4. Place the chicken on a roasting rack in a roasting pan. Arrange the carrots and potatoes around the chicken.

5. Roast the chicken for 1.5 hours, or until the internal temperature reaches 165°F and the skin is golden and crispy.

6. Let the chicken rest for 10 minutes before carving. Serve with the roasted vegetables.

Shepherd's Pie

Ingredients

- 1 lb ground lamb or beef
- 1 onion, chopped
- 2 carrots, diced
- 2 cloves garlic, minced
- 1 cup frozen peas
- 1 cup beef broth
- 1 tbsp tomato paste
- 2 tbsp Worcestershire sauce
- 2 tbsp flour
- 4 cups mashed potatoes (prepared in advance)
- Salt and pepper to taste

Instructions

1. Preheat the oven to 375°F.
2. In a large skillet, cook the ground lamb (or beef) over medium heat until browned. Drain any excess fat.
3. Add the onion, carrots, and garlic to the skillet and cook for 5-7 minutes, until softened.
4. Stir in the flour and cook for 2 minutes. Then add the tomato paste, Worcestershire sauce, and beef broth. Simmer for 10 minutes, until the mixture

thickens.

5. Stir in the peas and season with salt and pepper.

6. Transfer the meat mixture to a baking dish. Spread the mashed potatoes on top in an even layer.

7. Bake for 25-30 minutes, until the top is golden brown. Serve hot.

Cornbread and Chili

Ingredients for Chili:

- 1 lb ground beef
- 1 onion, chopped
- 2 cloves garlic, minced
- 1 can (15 oz) kidney beans, drained
- 1 can (15 oz) black beans, drained
- 1 can (14.5 oz) diced tomatoes
- 1 tbsp chili powder
- 1 tsp cumin
- 1/2 tsp smoked paprika
- Salt and pepper to taste

Ingredients for Cornbread:

- 1 cup cornmeal
- 1 cup all-purpose flour
- 1/4 cup sugar
- 1 tbsp baking powder
- 1/2 tsp salt
- 1 cup milk

- 2 eggs

- 1/4 cup melted butter

Instructions for Chili:

1. In a large pot, cook the ground beef over medium heat until browned. Drain excess fat.

2. Add the onion and garlic and cook for 5 minutes until softened.

3. Stir in the chili powder, cumin, paprika, salt, pepper, diced tomatoes, kidney beans, and black beans. Simmer for 30 minutes, stirring occasionally.

4. Adjust seasoning as needed and serve hot.

Instructions for Cornbread:

1. Preheat the oven to 375°F. Grease a 9-inch square baking dish.

2. In a large bowl, combine the cornmeal, flour, sugar, baking powder, and salt.

3. In a separate bowl, whisk together the milk, eggs, and melted butter.

4. Stir the wet ingredients into the dry ingredients until just combined.

5. Pour the batter into the prepared baking dish and bake for 20-25 minutes, or until golden brown.

6. Serve the chili with a side of warm cornbread.

Vegetable Minestrone

Ingredients

- 1 tbsp olive oil
- 1 onion, chopped
- 2 cloves garlic, minced
- 2 carrots, sliced
- 2 celery stalks, chopped
- 1 zucchini, diced
- 1 can (14.5 oz) diced tomatoes
- 4 cups vegetable broth
- 1 can (15 oz) kidney beans, drained
- 1 cup small pasta (like elbow macaroni)
- 1 cup spinach, chopped
- Salt and pepper to taste
- Fresh basil for garnish

Instructions

1. Heat the olive oil in a large pot over medium heat. Add the onion, garlic, carrots, and celery, cooking for 5-7 minutes until softened.

2. Add the zucchini, diced tomatoes, vegetable broth, kidney beans, and pasta. Bring to a boil, then reduce heat and simmer for 15-20 minutes, until the pasta is tender.

3. Stir in the spinach and cook for an additional 2-3 minutes.

4. Season with salt and pepper to taste. Garnish with fresh basil and serve hot.

Creamy Butternut Squash Soup

Ingredients

- 1 medium butternut squash, peeled, seeded, and cubed
- 1 onion, chopped
- 2 cloves garlic, minced
- 4 cups vegetable broth
- 1/2 cup heavy cream
- 2 tbsp olive oil
- Salt and pepper to taste
- Fresh thyme for garnish

Instructions

1. Preheat the oven to 400°F. Toss the butternut squash cubes with olive oil, salt, and pepper. Roast for 25-30 minutes, until tender.
2. In a large pot, sauté the onion and garlic over medium heat until softened, about 5 minutes.
3. Add the roasted squash and vegetable broth to the pot. Bring to a boil, then reduce the heat and simmer for 10 minutes.
4. Use an immersion blender to blend the soup until smooth, or carefully blend in batches using a regular blender.
5. Stir in the heavy cream and season with salt and pepper to taste.
6. Garnish with fresh thyme and serve hot.

Clam Chowder

Ingredients

- 2 tbsp butter
- 1 onion, chopped
- 2 cloves garlic, minced
- 2 celery stalks, chopped
- 2 cups potatoes, peeled and diced
- 2 cups chicken broth
- 2 cups heavy cream
- 2 cans (6.5 oz each) clams, drained, juice reserved
- Salt and pepper to taste
- Fresh parsley for garnish

Instructions

1. In a large pot, melt the butter over medium heat. Add the onion, garlic, and celery and cook until softened, about 5 minutes.
2. Add the potatoes and chicken broth. Bring to a boil, then reduce the heat and simmer for 15 minutes, until the potatoes are tender.
3. Stir in the heavy cream, clams, and reserved clam juice. Cook for an additional 5 minutes.
4. Season with salt and pepper to taste. Garnish with fresh parsley and serve hot.

Baked Potato Soup

Ingredients

- 4 large russet potatoes, peeled and diced
- 1/2 cup butter
- 1 onion, chopped
- 2 cloves garlic, minced
- 4 cups chicken broth
- 2 cups heavy cream
- 1/2 tsp salt
- 1/4 tsp black pepper
- 1/2 tsp paprika
- 1 cup shredded cheddar cheese
- 1/4 cup green onions, sliced
- 1/2 cup crispy bacon, crumbled (optional)

Instructions

1. Cook the diced potatoes in a large pot of boiling salted water for about 10-12 minutes, or until fork-tender. Drain and set aside.
2. In the same pot, melt butter over medium heat. Add the chopped onion and garlic, cooking for about 5 minutes until softened.
3. Stir in the chicken broth, cream, salt, pepper, and paprika. Bring to a simmer.

4. Add the cooked potatoes to the pot and mash some of them to thicken the soup.

5. Simmer for 10 minutes, then stir in shredded cheddar cheese until melted and smooth.

6. Top with sliced green onions and crumbled bacon before serving.

Chicken Tortilla Soup

Ingredients

- 1 lb chicken breasts, cooked and shredded
- 1 tbsp olive oil
- 1 onion, chopped
- 2 cloves garlic, minced
- 1 can (14.5 oz) diced tomatoes
- 1 can (15 oz) black beans, drained and rinsed
- 1 can (15 oz) corn kernels, drained
- 4 cups chicken broth
- 1 tbsp chili powder
- 1 tsp cumin
- 1/2 tsp paprika
- Salt and pepper to taste
- Tortilla chips, crushed
- Fresh cilantro, chopped
- Lime wedges
- Shredded cheese and sour cream (optional)

Instructions

1. In a large pot, heat olive oil over medium heat. Add the onion and garlic, cooking until softened, about 5 minutes.

2. Stir in the diced tomatoes, black beans, corn, chicken broth, chili powder, cumin, paprika, salt, and pepper.

3. Bring to a boil, then reduce the heat and simmer for 15 minutes.

4. Add the shredded chicken and cook for an additional 5 minutes.

5. Serve the soup with crushed tortilla chips, fresh cilantro, lime wedges, and optional toppings like cheese and sour cream.

Pulled Pork Sandwiches

Ingredients

- 2 lbs pork shoulder
- 1 onion, chopped
- 3 cloves garlic, minced
- 1 cup BBQ sauce
- 1/2 cup apple cider vinegar
- 1/2 cup chicken broth
- 1 tbsp brown sugar
- 1 tsp smoked paprika
- Salt and pepper to taste
- Burger buns
- Coleslaw (optional)

Instructions

1. In a slow cooker, combine the pork shoulder, chopped onion, garlic, BBQ sauce, apple cider vinegar, chicken broth, brown sugar, smoked paprika, salt, and pepper.
2. Cook on low for 8 hours or until the pork is tender and shreds easily.
3. Remove the pork from the slow cooker and shred it with two forks.
4. Return the shredded pork to the sauce and stir to coat.
5. Serve the pulled pork on buns with optional coleslaw.

Beef and Vegetable Stir-Fry

Ingredients

- 1 lb flank steak, thinly sliced
- 2 tbsp soy sauce
- 1 tbsp oyster sauce
- 1 tbsp hoisin sauce
- 1 tbsp sesame oil
- 1 tbsp vegetable oil
- 1 onion, sliced
- 1 bell pepper, sliced
- 1 zucchini, sliced
- 1 cup snap peas
- 2 cloves garlic, minced
- 1 tsp fresh ginger, grated
- Cooked rice for serving

Instructions

1. In a small bowl, mix the soy sauce, oyster sauce, hoisin sauce, and sesame oil to create the sauce.

2. Heat vegetable oil in a large skillet or wok over medium-high heat. Add the sliced beef and cook for 3-4 minutes until browned. Remove the beef and set aside.

3. In the same pan, add the onion, bell pepper, zucchini, snap peas, garlic, and ginger. Stir-fry for about 5 minutes until the vegetables are tender-crisp.

4. Return the beef to the pan and pour in the sauce. Stir to coat the beef and vegetables in the sauce and cook for an additional 2-3 minutes.

5. Serve over cooked rice.

Meatball Soup

Ingredients

- 1 lb ground beef
- 1/4 cup breadcrumbs
- 1/4 cup grated Parmesan cheese
- 1 egg
- 2 tbsp fresh parsley, chopped
- 2 cloves garlic, minced
- 4 cups beef broth
- 1 can (14.5 oz) diced tomatoes
- 2 carrots, sliced
- 2 celery stalks, chopped
- 1 onion, chopped
- 1 tsp dried oregano
- Salt and pepper to taste

Instructions

1. In a bowl, combine the ground beef, breadcrumbs, Parmesan cheese, egg, parsley, garlic, salt, and pepper. Shape into small meatballs.

2. In a large pot, bring the beef broth, diced tomatoes, carrots, celery, onion, and oregano to a boil.

3. Add the meatballs to the soup, reduce the heat, and simmer for 20-25 minutes, until the meatballs are cooked through.

4. Serve hot, garnished with extra parsley if desired.

Beef Stroganoff

Ingredients

- 1 lb beef sirloin or tenderloin, thinly sliced
- 2 tbsp butter
- 1 onion, chopped
- 2 cloves garlic, minced
- 2 cups beef broth
- 1 cup sour cream
- 1 tbsp Dijon mustard
- 2 tbsp flour
- Salt and pepper to taste
- 1 tbsp fresh parsley, chopped
- Cooked egg noodles for serving

Instructions

1. In a large skillet, melt butter over medium-high heat. Add the beef and cook until browned, about 3-4 minutes. Remove and set aside.
2. In the same skillet, add the onion and garlic, cooking for 5 minutes until softened.
3. Stir in the flour and cook for 1 minute to form a roux.
4. Gradually add the beef broth, whisking constantly to avoid lumps. Bring to a simmer and cook until the sauce thickens, about 5 minutes.

5. Stir in the sour cream, Dijon mustard, salt, and pepper. Add the beef back to the skillet and cook for an additional 3-4 minutes.

6. Serve over cooked egg noodles, garnished with fresh parsley.

Beef and Barley Soup

Ingredients

- 1 lb beef stew meat, cubed
- 2 tbsp olive oil
- 1 onion, chopped
- 2 carrots, sliced
- 2 celery stalks, chopped
- 2 cloves garlic, minced
- 6 cups beef broth
- 1 cup barley
- 1 tsp thyme
- 1 bay leaf
- Salt and pepper to taste

Instructions

1. Heat olive oil in a large pot over medium heat. Add the beef stew meat and cook until browned, about 5 minutes. Remove the beef and set aside.

2. In the same pot, add the onion, carrots, celery, and garlic. Cook for 5-7 minutes until softened.

3. Stir in the beef broth, barley, thyme, bay leaf, and beef. Bring to a boil, then reduce the heat and simmer for 45 minutes, or until the barley is tender.

4. Season with salt and pepper to taste, then serve hot.

Sweet Potato and Black Bean Chili

Ingredients

- 2 tbsp olive oil
- 1 onion, chopped
- 2 cloves garlic, minced
- 2 sweet potatoes, peeled and diced
- 1 can (15 oz) black beans, drained
- 1 can (14.5 oz) diced tomatoes
- 1 can (15 oz) corn kernels, drained
- 1 tbsp chili powder
- 1 tsp cumin
- 1/2 tsp smoked paprika
- Salt and pepper to taste
- 2 cups vegetable broth
- Fresh cilantro for garnish

Instructions

1. Heat olive oil in a large pot over medium heat. Add the onion and garlic, cooking until softened, about 5 minutes.

2. Add the sweet potatoes, black beans, diced tomatoes, corn, chili powder, cumin, paprika, salt, and pepper.

3. Pour in the vegetable broth and bring to a boil. Reduce the heat and simmer for 25-30 minutes, until the sweet potatoes are tender.

4. Serve hot, garnished with fresh cilantro.

Sausage and Pepper Skillet

Ingredients

- 1 lb Italian sausage, sliced
- 1 tbsp olive oil
- 1 onion, sliced
- 2 bell peppers, sliced (use different colors for variety)
- 2 cloves garlic, minced
- 1/2 tsp red pepper flakes (optional)
- Salt and pepper to taste
- 1/4 cup fresh parsley, chopped (for garnish)

Instructions

1. In a large skillet, heat olive oil over medium-high heat. Add the sausage slices and cook until browned on both sides, about 5-7 minutes. Remove and set aside.
2. In the same skillet, add the sliced onion and bell peppers. Cook, stirring occasionally, until the vegetables are soft and slightly caramelized, about 8-10 minutes.
3. Add the minced garlic and red pepper flakes (if using), and cook for another 1-2 minutes until fragrant.
4. Return the sausage to the skillet, toss everything together, and cook for another 2-3 minutes to heat through.
5. Season with salt and pepper to taste, and garnish with fresh parsley before serving.

Chicken Alfredo

Ingredients

- 2 boneless, skinless chicken breasts
- 2 tbsp olive oil
- 1/2 tsp salt
- 1/4 tsp black pepper
- 2 cups heavy cream
- 1/2 cup grated Parmesan cheese
- 3 cloves garlic, minced
- 1 lb fettuccine pasta
- 1 tbsp fresh parsley, chopped (for garnish)

Instructions

1. Heat olive oil in a large skillet over medium-high heat. Season the chicken breasts with salt and pepper, then cook them in the skillet for about 6-7 minutes per side, until cooked through. Remove the chicken and set aside.
2. In the same skillet, add the minced garlic and sauté for 1-2 minutes until fragrant.
3. Add the heavy cream to the skillet and bring it to a simmer. Stir in the Parmesan cheese and cook, stirring, until the sauce has thickened, about 3-5 minutes.
4. Meanwhile, cook the fettuccine pasta according to package instructions, then drain.
5. Slice the cooked chicken into strips and add it to the skillet with the Alfredo sauce. Toss in the cooked pasta, coating everything evenly with the sauce.

6. Garnish with fresh parsley and serve immediately.

Chicken and Rice Casserole

Ingredients

- 2 cups cooked chicken, shredded
- 1 cup rice (white or brown)
- 1 can (10.5 oz) cream of chicken soup
- 1/2 cup sour cream
- 1/2 cup shredded cheddar cheese
- 1/2 cup frozen peas
- 1/2 cup diced carrots
- 1/2 tsp garlic powder
- 1/2 tsp onion powder
- Salt and pepper to taste

Instructions

1. Preheat your oven to 350°F (175°C). Grease a 9x13-inch baking dish.
2. In a large mixing bowl, combine the cooked chicken, cooked rice, cream of chicken soup, sour cream, shredded cheddar cheese, peas, carrots, garlic powder, onion powder, salt, and pepper.
3. Stir until everything is well mixed, then transfer the mixture to the prepared baking dish.
4. Cover with foil and bake for 25-30 minutes. Remove the foil, stir, and bake for an additional 10 minutes until the casserole is bubbly and golden on top.

5. Let cool for a few minutes before serving.

Beef and Mushroom Pie

Ingredients

- 1 lb ground beef
- 1 cup mushrooms, sliced
- 1 onion, chopped
- 2 cloves garlic, minced
- 1 tbsp tomato paste
- 1 tbsp Worcestershire sauce
- 1/2 cup beef broth
- 1/4 cup flour
- 1/2 tsp thyme
- 1/2 tsp salt
- 1/4 tsp black pepper
- 1 sheet puff pastry
- 1 egg (for egg wash)

Instructions

1. Preheat your oven to 375°F (190°C).

2. In a large skillet, cook the ground beef over medium-high heat until browned. Remove any excess fat and set the beef aside.

3. In the same skillet, add the mushrooms and cook for 5-7 minutes until they release their moisture and begin to brown.

4. Add the chopped onion and minced garlic, cooking for another 3-4 minutes until softened.

5. Stir in the tomato paste, Worcestershire sauce, beef broth, flour, thyme, salt, and pepper. Cook until the mixture thickens, about 5 minutes.

6. Return the beef to the skillet and mix everything together. Remove from heat.

7. Roll out the puff pastry to fit your baking dish. Transfer the beef and mushroom mixture into the dish, then top with the puff pastry.

8. Brush the pastry with a beaten egg for a golden finish.

9. Bake for 25-30 minutes until the pastry is golden and puffed.

10. Let cool for a few minutes before serving.

Stuffed Bell Peppers

Ingredients

- 4 large bell peppers, tops cut off and seeds removed
- 1 lb ground beef or turkey
- 1 cup cooked rice
- 1 can (15 oz) tomato sauce
- 1 tsp garlic powder
- 1/2 tsp onion powder
- 1/2 tsp cumin
- 1/4 tsp chili powder
- 1/2 cup shredded cheese (cheddar or mozzarella)
- Salt and pepper to taste

Instructions

1. Preheat your oven to 375°F (190°C).
2. In a skillet, cook the ground beef or turkey over medium-high heat until browned. Drain excess fat.
3. Stir in the cooked rice, tomato sauce, garlic powder, onion powder, cumin, chili powder, salt, and pepper. Mix well and cook for 5 minutes.
4. Stuff the bell peppers with the meat mixture, packing it tightly.
5. Place the stuffed peppers in a baking dish and cover with foil.

6. Bake for 25 minutes, then remove the foil and sprinkle cheese on top of each pepper.

7. Return to the oven and bake for an additional 5-10 minutes until the cheese is melted and bubbly.

8. Serve hot.

Chicken and Wild Rice Soup

Ingredients

- 1 lb chicken breast, cooked and shredded
- 1/2 cup wild rice
- 1/2 cup carrots, diced
- 1/2 cup celery, diced
- 1 onion, chopped
- 3 cloves garlic, minced
- 6 cups chicken broth
- 1/2 tsp thyme
- 1/2 tsp rosemary
- 1/2 cup heavy cream
- Salt and pepper to taste

Instructions

1. In a large pot, combine the chicken broth, carrots, celery, onion, garlic, wild rice, thyme, and rosemary. Bring to a boil, then reduce the heat and simmer for 30-35 minutes until the rice is tender.
2. Add the shredded chicken to the soup and cook for an additional 5-7 minutes.
3. Stir in the heavy cream and season with salt and pepper to taste.
4. Serve hot.

Lasagna Soup

Ingredients

- 1 lb ground beef or sausage
- 1 onion, chopped
- 2 cloves garlic, minced
- 1 can (14.5 oz) diced tomatoes
- 1 can (6 oz) tomato paste
- 4 cups beef broth
- 2 tsp Italian seasoning
- 1/2 tsp red pepper flakes (optional)
- 8 oz lasagna noodles, broken into pieces
- 1/2 cup ricotta cheese
- 1/2 cup shredded mozzarella cheese
- Fresh basil for garnish

Instructions

1. In a large pot, cook the ground beef or sausage over medium heat until browned. Add the onion and garlic, cooking until softened.
2. Stir in the diced tomatoes, tomato paste, beef broth, Italian seasoning, and red pepper flakes. Bring to a simmer and cook for 10 minutes.
3. Add the broken lasagna noodles and cook for 10-12 minutes, until tender.

4. Stir in the ricotta and mozzarella cheese, then cook for 2-3 minutes until the cheese is melted and the soup is creamy.

5. Serve hot, garnished with fresh basil.

Spaghetti Carbonara

Ingredients

- 12 oz spaghetti
- 1/2 lb pancetta or bacon, diced
- 3 large eggs
- 1/2 cup Parmesan cheese, grated
- 1/4 cup heavy cream (optional)
- 2 cloves garlic, minced
- Salt and black pepper to taste

Instructions

1. Cook the spaghetti according to package instructions, reserving 1 cup of pasta cooking water.
2. In a skillet, cook the pancetta or bacon over medium heat until crispy. Remove from the skillet and set aside.
3. In a mixing bowl, whisk together the eggs, Parmesan cheese, heavy cream (if using), and a pinch of black pepper.
4. Add the cooked spaghetti to the skillet with the pancetta, tossing to coat in the rendered fat. Remove from heat.
5. Slowly pour the egg mixture over the pasta, tossing quickly to create a creamy sauce. Add reserved pasta water as needed to adjust the consistency.
6. Season with additional salt and pepper to taste, and serve immediately.

Pork Tenderloin with Apples

Ingredients

- 1 lb pork tenderloin
- 2 tbsp olive oil
- 1 onion, sliced
- 2 apples, peeled and sliced
- 1/2 cup apple cider
- 1/2 tsp cinnamon
- Salt and pepper to taste

Instructions

1. Preheat your oven to 400°F (200°C).
2. Heat olive oil in an oven-safe skillet over medium-high heat. Season the pork tenderloin with salt, pepper, and cinnamon, then sear on all sides for 5-7 minutes until browned.
3. Remove the pork from the skillet and set aside. In the same skillet, add the sliced onion and apples. Cook for 5 minutes until softened.
4. Add the apple cider and return the pork to the skillet.
5. Transfer the skillet to the oven and roast for 20-25 minutes, or until the pork reaches an internal temperature of 145°F (63°C).
6. Let the pork rest for a few minutes before slicing and serving with the apples and onions.

Risotto with Parmesan and Mushrooms

Ingredients

- 1 cup Arborio rice
- 1 tbsp olive oil
- 1 small onion, chopped
- 2 cloves garlic, minced
- 1 cup mushrooms, sliced
- 4 cups chicken or vegetable broth, warm
- 1/2 cup dry white wine
- 1/2 cup grated Parmesan cheese
- 2 tbsp butter
- Salt and pepper to taste
- Fresh parsley for garnish (optional)

Instructions

1. In a large skillet or saucepan, heat the olive oil over medium heat. Add the onion and cook for about 3-4 minutes until softened.

2. Add the garlic and mushrooms, cooking for another 5-7 minutes until the mushrooms release their moisture and begin to brown.

3. Stir in the Arborio rice and cook for 1-2 minutes until the rice is slightly toasted.

4. Add the white wine and stir until it is mostly absorbed.

5. Gradually add the warm broth, one ladleful at a time, stirring constantly and allowing the liquid to be absorbed before adding more. Continue this process until the rice is tender and creamy, about 20-25 minutes.

6. Once the rice is cooked, stir in the butter and Parmesan cheese. Season with salt and pepper to taste.

7. Garnish with fresh parsley before serving.

Chicken Parmesan

Ingredients

- 4 boneless, skinless chicken breasts
- 1 cup flour
- 2 large eggs, beaten
- 1 cup breadcrumbs
- 1/2 cup grated Parmesan cheese
- 2 cups marinara sauce
- 1 1/2 cups shredded mozzarella cheese
- 2 tbsp olive oil
- Salt and pepper to taste
- Fresh basil for garnish (optional)

Instructions

1. Preheat your oven to 375°F (190°C). Grease a baking dish with cooking spray or olive oil.

2. Season the chicken breasts with salt and pepper. Dredge each chicken breast in flour, then dip in the beaten eggs, and coat in a mixture of breadcrumbs and Parmesan cheese.

3. In a large skillet, heat the olive oil over medium-high heat. Cook the breaded chicken breasts for 4-5 minutes per side until golden brown. Transfer the chicken to the prepared baking dish.

4. Spoon marinara sauce over each chicken breast, then top with shredded mozzarella cheese.

5. Bake in the oven for 20-25 minutes until the chicken is cooked through (internal temperature should be 165°F).

6. Garnish with fresh basil and serve.

Baked Macaroni and Cheese

Ingredients

- 1 lb elbow macaroni
- 2 tbsp butter
- 2 tbsp all-purpose flour
- 2 cups milk
- 2 cups shredded cheddar cheese
- 1/2 cup grated Parmesan cheese
- Salt and pepper to taste
- 1/2 cup breadcrumbs (optional for topping)

Instructions

1. Preheat your oven to 350°F (175°C). Grease a 9x13-inch baking dish.
2. Cook the macaroni according to the package instructions, then drain and set aside.
3. In a large saucepan, melt the butter over medium heat. Stir in the flour and cook for 1-2 minutes until it forms a roux.
4. Gradually whisk in the milk, cooking and stirring until the sauce thickens, about 5 minutes.
5. Stir in the cheddar cheese and Parmesan cheese, and cook until melted and smooth. Season with salt and pepper to taste.
6. Combine the cooked macaroni with the cheese sauce, then pour the mixture into the prepared baking dish.

7. (Optional) Sprinkle breadcrumbs on top for a crunchy topping. Bake for 20-25 minutes until the top is golden and bubbly.

Fish Tacos with Cilantro Lime Rice

Ingredients

- 1 lb white fish fillets (such as tilapia or cod)
- 1 tbsp olive oil
- 1 tsp paprika
- 1/2 tsp cumin
- 1/4 tsp chili powder
- Salt and pepper to taste
- 8 small corn or flour tortillas
- 1 cup rice
- 1 1/2 cups water
- 1 tbsp lime juice
- 1/4 cup fresh cilantro, chopped
- 1/4 cup sour cream
- 1 tbsp lime juice (for topping)
- 1/2 cup shredded cabbage (for topping)
- Salsa (optional)

Instructions

1. In a small bowl, mix the paprika, cumin, chili powder, salt, and pepper. Rub the seasoning mix over the fish fillets.

2. Heat olive oil in a large skillet over medium-high heat. Cook the fish fillets for 3-4 minutes per side, until cooked through and flaky. Remove from heat and set aside.

3. In a medium saucepan, combine the rice and water. Bring to a boil, then reduce to a simmer and cover. Cook for 18-20 minutes, until the rice is tender.

4. Fluff the rice with a fork and stir in lime juice and chopped cilantro.

5. Warm the tortillas in a skillet or microwave. Assemble the tacos by placing a portion of the fish on each tortilla, followed by a spoonful of cilantro lime rice, a drizzle of sour cream, a squeeze of lime juice, and a sprinkle of shredded cabbage. Add salsa if desired.

6. Serve immediately.

Spicy Sausage Soup

Ingredients

- 1 lb spicy Italian sausage, casings removed
- 1 onion, chopped
- 2 cloves garlic, minced
- 1 can (14.5 oz) diced tomatoes
- 1 can (15 oz) cannellini beans, drained and rinsed
- 4 cups chicken broth
- 2 cups kale, chopped
- 1/2 tsp red pepper flakes (optional for extra spice)
- Salt and pepper to taste
- 1/2 cup heavy cream

Instructions

1. In a large pot, cook the sausage over medium heat, breaking it up with a spoon until browned, about 5-7 minutes.
2. Add the chopped onion and garlic, cooking for 3-4 minutes until softened.
3. Stir in the diced tomatoes, cannellini beans, chicken broth, and kale. Bring to a simmer and cook for 10-15 minutes, until the flavors have melded together.
4. Stir in the heavy cream and season with red pepper flakes, salt, and pepper to taste.
5. Serve hot.

Braised Short Ribs

Ingredients

- 4 beef short ribs
- 2 tbsp olive oil
- Salt and pepper to taste
- 1 onion, chopped
- 2 carrots, chopped
- 2 celery stalks, chopped
- 2 cloves garlic, minced
- 1 cup red wine
- 2 cups beef broth
- 1 tsp thyme
- 2 bay leaves

Instructions

1. Preheat your oven to 350°F (175°C).

2. Season the short ribs with salt and pepper. Heat olive oil in a large Dutch oven over medium-high heat. Brown the short ribs on all sides, about 5 minutes. Remove the ribs and set aside.

3. In the same pot, add the chopped onion, carrots, and celery. Cook for 5-7 minutes until softened.

4. Add the garlic and cook for another minute.

5. Pour in the red wine and cook for 3-4 minutes, scraping up any browned bits from the bottom of the pot.

6. Return the short ribs to the pot and add the beef broth, thyme, and bay leaves.

7. Cover the pot with a lid and transfer it to the oven. Braise for 2 1/2 to 3 hours, until the meat is tender and falls off the bone.

8. Serve the short ribs with the braising liquid and vegetables.

Cajun Jambalaya

Ingredients

- 1 lb andouille sausage, sliced
- 1 lb chicken breast, diced
- 1 onion, chopped
- 1 bell pepper, chopped
- 2 cloves garlic, minced
- 1 can (14.5 oz) diced tomatoes
- 1 1/2 cups long-grain rice
- 3 cups chicken broth
- 1 tbsp Cajun seasoning
- 1/2 tsp thyme
- Salt and pepper to taste
- 1/4 cup green onions, chopped (for garnish)

Instructions

1. In a large pot, cook the sausage over medium heat for 5-7 minutes until browned. Remove and set aside.
2. In the same pot, cook the diced chicken breast until browned on all sides, about 5-7 minutes.
3. Add the chopped onion, bell pepper, and garlic, cooking until softened, about 5 minutes.

4. Stir in the diced tomatoes, rice, chicken broth, Cajun seasoning, thyme, salt, and pepper. Bring to a boil.

5. Reduce the heat to low, cover, and simmer for 20-25 minutes, until the rice is cooked and the liquid has been absorbed.

6. Garnish with green onions and serve.

Chili Mac

Ingredients

- 1 lb ground beef
- 1 onion, chopped
- 2 cloves garlic, minced
- 1 can (15 oz) kidney beans, drained and rinsed
- 1 can (15 oz) tomato sauce
- 1 tbsp chili powder
- 1 tsp cumin
- 1/2 tsp paprika
- 1 cup elbow macaroni
- 1/2 cup shredded cheddar cheese
- Salt and pepper to taste

Instructions

1. In a large pot, cook the ground beef over medium heat until browned, about 5-7 minutes. Drain any excess fat.
2. Add the chopped onion and garlic, cooking until softened, about 3 minutes.
3. Stir in the kidney beans, tomato sauce, chili powder, cumin, and paprika. Season with salt and pepper.
4. Add the macaroni and enough water to cover the mixture. Bring to a boil, then reduce to a simmer. Cook for 10-12 minutes, until the pasta is tender and the

sauce thickens.

5. Stir in the shredded cheddar cheese and serve.

Chicken and Sweet Potato Skillet

Ingredients

- 2 chicken breasts, sliced
- 2 sweet potatoes, peeled and diced
- 1 tbsp olive oil
- 1 tsp paprika
- 1/2 tsp cumin
- 1/2 tsp cinnamon
- Salt and pepper to taste
- 1/4 cup fresh parsley, chopped

Instructions

1. Heat olive oil in a large skillet over medium heat. Add the diced sweet potatoes and cook for 8-10 minutes, stirring occasionally, until tender.
2. Season the chicken with paprika, cumin, cinnamon, salt, and pepper.
3. Push the sweet potatoes to one side of the skillet, then add the chicken to the other side. Cook for 5-7 minutes per side, until the chicken is cooked through.
4. Toss everything together, then garnish with fresh parsley and serve.

Beef and Potato Casserole

Ingredients

- 1 lb ground beef
- 4 medium potatoes, peeled and thinly sliced
- 1 onion, chopped
- 2 cloves garlic, minced
- 2 cups shredded cheddar cheese
- 1 cup sour cream
- Salt and pepper to taste
- 1/2 tsp paprika

Instructions

1. Preheat your oven to 375°F (190°C). Grease a 9x13-inch baking dish.
2. Cook the ground beef in a skillet over medium heat until browned, about 5-7 minutes. Drain any excess fat.
3. Add the chopped onion and garlic to the beef, cooking for 3-4 minutes until softened.
4. Layer the sliced potatoes in the prepared baking dish, then top with the beef mixture.
5. Combine the sour cream, paprika, salt, and pepper, then spread over the beef mixture.
6. Sprinkle shredded cheddar cheese on top and bake for 35-40 minutes, until the potatoes are tender and the cheese is melted.

Shrimp Scampi

Ingredients

- 1 lb large shrimp, peeled and deveined
- 8 oz spaghetti or linguine
- 4 tbsp butter
- 2 tbsp olive oil
- 4 cloves garlic, minced
- 1/4 tsp red pepper flakes (optional)
- 1/2 cup dry white wine
- Juice of 1 lemon
- 1/4 cup fresh parsley, chopped
- Salt and pepper to taste

Instructions

1. Cook the pasta according to package instructions, drain, and set aside, reserving some pasta water.

2. In a large skillet, melt the butter and olive oil over medium heat. Add the garlic and red pepper flakes (if using) and sauté for about 1 minute until fragrant.

3. Add the shrimp to the skillet and cook for 2-3 minutes per side, until they turn pink and are cooked through. Season with salt and pepper.

4. Remove the shrimp from the skillet and set aside. Add the white wine and lemon juice to the skillet, scraping up any browned bits from the bottom of the pan.

5. Add the cooked pasta to the skillet and toss to coat in the sauce. If the pasta seems dry, add a little reserved pasta water.

6. Return the shrimp to the skillet and toss everything together. Garnish with fresh parsley and serve immediately.

Vegetable Curry

Ingredients

- 1 tbsp olive oil
- 1 onion, chopped
- 2 cloves garlic, minced
- 1 tbsp grated ginger
- 1 tbsp curry powder
- 1 can (14 oz) coconut milk
- 2 cups vegetable broth
- 1 cup carrots, sliced
- 1 cup bell peppers, chopped
- 1 cup zucchini, chopped
- 1 can (15 oz) chickpeas, drained and rinsed
- 1/2 cup spinach (optional)
- Salt and pepper to taste
- Cooked rice for serving

Instructions

1. Heat olive oil in a large pot over medium heat. Add the onion and cook for 5 minutes until softened.

2. Add the garlic, ginger, and curry powder, and cook for another minute until fragrant.

3. Stir in the coconut milk and vegetable broth. Bring to a simmer.

4. Add the carrots, bell peppers, zucchini, and chickpeas. Simmer for 15-20 minutes, until the vegetables are tender.

5. Stir in the spinach (if using) and cook for an additional 2 minutes until wilted.

6. Season with salt and pepper to taste, and serve over cooked rice.

Meatball Sub Sandwiches

Ingredients

- 1 lb ground beef
- 1/4 cup breadcrumbs
- 1/4 cup grated Parmesan cheese
- 1 egg
- 2 cloves garlic, minced
- 1/2 tsp dried oregano
- 1/2 tsp dried basil
- 1/4 tsp salt
- 1/4 tsp pepper
- 1 cup marinara sauce
- 4 sub rolls
- 1 1/2 cups shredded mozzarella cheese

Instructions

1. Preheat your oven to 375°F (190°C).
2. In a large bowl, mix the ground beef, breadcrumbs, Parmesan cheese, egg, garlic, oregano, basil, salt, and pepper. Form the mixture into 12 meatballs.
3. In a skillet, heat some olive oil over medium heat. Brown the meatballs on all sides, about 5 minutes. Then transfer the meatballs to a baking dish.

4. Pour marinara sauce over the meatballs and bake in the oven for 20-25 minutes, until the meatballs are cooked through.

5. Split the sub rolls and place them on a baking sheet. Toast in the oven for about 5 minutes.

6. Remove the meatballs from the sauce, and place 3 meatballs in each sub roll. Top with marinara sauce and shredded mozzarella cheese.

7. Return the sandwiches to the oven and bake for an additional 5-7 minutes, until the cheese is melted and bubbly.

Eggplant Parmesan

Ingredients

- 2 medium eggplants, sliced into 1/2-inch rounds
- 2 cups marinara sauce
- 2 cups breadcrumbs
- 1 cup grated Parmesan cheese
- 1/2 cup all-purpose flour
- 2 eggs, beaten
- 2 cups shredded mozzarella cheese
- 1/4 cup fresh basil, chopped
- Olive oil for frying
- Salt and pepper to taste

Instructions

1. Preheat your oven to 375°F (190°C). Grease a 9x13-inch baking dish with cooking spray.

2. Set up a breading station: In one bowl, place the flour. In a second bowl, beat the eggs. In a third bowl, combine breadcrumbs, Parmesan cheese, salt, and pepper.

3. Dip each eggplant slice first in flour, then in beaten egg, and finally coat with the breadcrumb mixture.

4. Heat a little olive oil in a large skillet over medium heat. Fry the eggplant slices for 2-3 minutes per side, until golden brown. Place fried eggplant on paper towels to drain excess oil.

5. In the prepared baking dish, spread a thin layer of marinara sauce on the bottom. Layer the fried eggplant slices on top, followed by more marinara sauce and a sprinkle of mozzarella cheese.

6. Repeat the layering process, finishing with a layer of cheese on top.

7. Bake in the oven for 25-30 minutes, until the cheese is melted and bubbly.

8. Garnish with fresh basil and serve.

Pork Carnitas

Ingredients

- 3 lbs pork shoulder, cut into large chunks
- 1 onion, quartered
- 4 cloves garlic, smashed
- 1 orange, cut in half
- 2 tbsp olive oil
- 1 tsp cumin
- 1 tsp chili powder
- 1/2 tsp oregano
- Salt and pepper to taste
- Tortillas for serving
- Fresh cilantro, chopped (for garnish)
- Lime wedges (for serving)

Instructions

1. In a large pot or Dutch oven, heat olive oil over medium-high heat. Season the pork shoulder with cumin, chili powder, oregano, salt, and pepper.
2. Brown the pork on all sides in the hot oil for about 5 minutes.
3. Add the onion, garlic, and orange halves to the pot. Pour in enough water to cover the pork, about 3 cups.

4. Bring the mixture to a simmer, then cover the pot and reduce the heat to low. Simmer for 2 1/2 to 3 hours, until the pork is tender and easily shreds.

5. Remove the pork from the pot and shred with two forks.

6. (Optional) For crispy carnitas, heat a little oil in a skillet over medium-high heat and crisp the shredded pork for 5-7 minutes, turning occasionally.

7. Serve the carnitas in warm tortillas, garnished with fresh cilantro and lime wedges.

Beef Tacos with Guacamole

Ingredients

- 1 lb ground beef
- 1 packet taco seasoning (or homemade seasoning)
- 1/2 cup water
- 8 small tortillas
- 1 cup shredded lettuce
- 1/2 cup diced tomatoes
- 1/2 cup shredded cheddar cheese
- 1/4 cup sour cream
- **For the Guacamole**:
    - 2 ripe avocados
    - 1 small lime, juiced
    - 1/4 cup diced onion
    - 1/2 cup chopped cilantro
    - Salt and pepper to taste

Instructions

1. In a skillet, cook the ground beef over medium heat until browned. Drain any excess fat.

2. Stir in the taco seasoning and water, and simmer for 5 minutes, until the beef is coated and the sauce has thickened.

3. For the guacamole, mash the avocados in a bowl. Stir in lime juice, onion, cilantro, salt, and pepper.

4. Warm the tortillas in a skillet or microwave. Assemble the tacos by filling each tortilla with seasoned beef, shredded lettuce, diced tomatoes, cheese, and a dollop of sour cream.

5. Top with guacamole and serve immediately.